JOB BASICS™
GETTING THE JOB YOU NEED

GETTING A JOB IN
THE CONSTRUCTION
INDUSTRY

PHILIP WOLNY

Published in 2017 by The Rosen Publishing Group, Inc.

29 East 21st Street, New York, NY 10010
Copyright © 2017 by The Rosen Publishing Group, Inc.

First Edition

Library of Congress Cataloging-in-Publication Data

Names: Wolny, Philip, author.
Title: Getting a job in the construction industry / Philip Wolny
Description: First edition. | New York : Rosen Publishing, 2017. | Series:
 Job basics: getting the job you need | Includes bibliographical references
 and index.
Identifiers: LCCN 2016008891 | ISBN 9781477785645 (library bound)
Subjects: LCSH: Construction industry—Vocational guidance—Juvenile
 literature. | Construction workers—Juvenile literature.
Classification: LCC TH159 .W65 2017 | DDC 624.023—dc23
LC record available at http://lccn.loc.gov/2016008891

Manufactured in China

CONTENTS

INTRODUCTION

The sounds of hammers pounding, saw blades whirring, and big machines moving earth are like music to your ears. You might enjoy taking apart common household items, and crafting small things for friends and family or useful items for your own personal use. You like structure and meeting deadlines. Seeing the physical results of doing hard, hands-on work is personally satisfying to you. Down the line, when you get older, you do not see yourself being completely satisfied in an office job—at least not a regular one.

If you relate to any of these, it is likely you may enjoy and thrive in an exciting, fulfilling, and often lucrative field: the construction industry. Construction is a key part of the United States' economy, and integral to economies around the world. It employs millions of men and women in the skilled trades, as laborers and management, and creates jobs and prosperity for numerous other related fields, including real estate development and management. It is responsible for the homes and apartments people dwell in, the offices and workplaces they use, and the public spaces they visit.

Working in construction is not for everyone. While there are administrative jobs in the industry, most of the people who work in this sector are attracted to it because they like to get their hands dirty at some point, so to speak. Those who are handy naturally are attracted to this kind of work. Being in good physical shape is a requirement, as is the willingness to often work long hours while physically exerting oneself.

Workers range in skill set from novices doing basic work like demolition or asbestos removal, to highly skilled and well-compensated tradespeople like metalworkers, electricians, and engineers, or managerial posts like construction or project manager.

Construction is a tough but rewarding job that requires teamwork, technical know-how, and often a fair amount of training, both in the classroom and on the job.

The wide variety of jobs that make up the construction field provide many options for getting hands-on. Carpenters, cement masons, electricians, drywallers, glaziers (glass workers), and stone and brick masons are a few of the many specialists employed on any given project.

With some timely advice (including this book), early instruction in basic shop classes in school or elsewhere, and training in a vocational-technical (vo-tech) institute or other accredited program, you will be ready for apprenticeships and the career ladder.

This book will provide the job basics necessary to get the wheels in motion. Besides exploring the construction sector and what jobs are available, it provides information on the education and training you will need. In addition, you will get a rundown of how to look for and expore job opportunities, and a few crucial bits of advice on how to craft your resume and have a great interview. With some elbow grease, preparation, and determination, a satisfying job in construction awaits you! Let's get started.

CHAPTER ONE

The Construction Industry

There are many ways to look at (and divide up) the construction industry. One way is to separate it between residential and nonresidential building—that is, between private homes and offices. Another way is between private projects and public works, like an office headquarters for a major corporation versus a new public library in your neighborhood.

Differences also remain among the construction of structures that house people or workers, and other projects, such as parking lots, subway tunnels, highways, oil rigs, port facilities, and much more. Construction work includes working on something from the ground up as well as renovating, repairing, or remodeling existing buildings, as well as demolishing and stripping down old and decaying buildings, especially to make way for new construction.

Is Construction the Right Career for You?

Many workers gravitate to the construction field as a livelihood and lifelong career for a few different reasons. While some people may take a construction job or two in their lifetimes and turn to other fields, for many it requires some

A roof worker carries a wooden beam as he helps complete the roof of a new home. Physical stamina and physical fitness are two necessary prerequisites for working hands-on in construction.

degree of early commitment, due to the necessary training, both in school and on the job.

Working with one's hands is a big draw. While such work can be physically demanding and sometimes even grueling, for many people this is a plus, not a minus. Using your muscles can be both physically and mentally satisfying. But, you will likely be in good shape.

Another attraction is actually seeing the products of your labor take shape. Office workers might complain sometimes that they feel detached from their work because they wonder what the point of it all is. With construction work, that is rarely an issue. Being able to physically touch something you have created, as well as knowing that others will benefit from it, can be pretty satisfying and inspiring.

Construction is never boring, and no two days or projects are ever quite the same. You may spend months on an office tower, and then be hired to help add on a section of a suburban home. The same time next year, you may be hanging off the side of a half-finished sports stadium. Variety is another big plus for construction workers. They can work indoors or outdoors, and

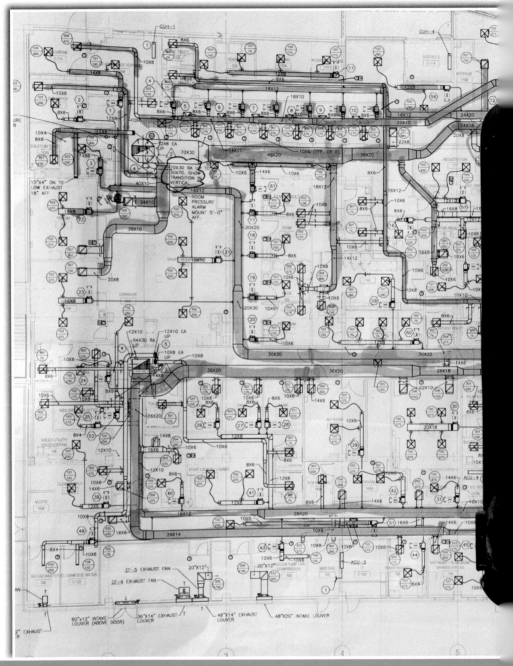

An iPad is shown alongside some building blueprints. One requirement for new construction workers in the twenty-first century will be to pair older technical knowledge with newer tools, such as tablets and architectural software.

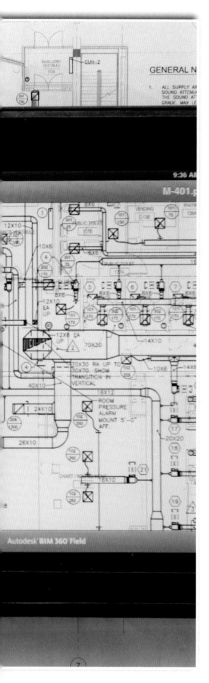

many people enjoy being able to periodically work outside, without office cubicles or walls.

Those who are handy and enjoy working in a technical capacity are also ideal candidates for the construction sector. While a majority of people rarely think of the wooden beams supporting the ceiling above them, or the intricate wiring feeding their computer and appliances power, construction workers are intimately familiar with how things work behind the scenes, and they use that knowledge daily.

The Demands of the Job

Besides the things that make construction interesting or appealing, there are also requirements, and even drawbacks. You must be able to balance these with the pluses.

In many construction jobs, the physical demands can be taxing. Workers can get pretty exhausted by the end of the day. They need to ensure they stretch properly and do not overexert themselves. Common pitfalls of some construction work include pulling muscles, throwing out one's back, scratches and scrapes, falls, and other mishaps.

Someone who is clumsy or reckless will not last long in construction—hopefully, because their bosses intervene, and not because they put themselves in the hospital or worse. If you know yourself well, you can make an educated guess about how well you would adjust to such a work environment.

Construction work can also be mentally stressful, too. In many jobs, you need to plan your work carefully and be prepared to react to changes in schedule and workload, and have troubleshooting abilities. Those who manage other workers in a crew, or group—usually called construction foremen—in particular need to be problem solvers. They must manage others and plan and execute their particular aspect of the job. On small jobs, they call the shots, while on larger ones they likely answer to construction managers or project managers above them. These, in turn, have even more responsibilities.

If you plan to rise in your chosen field, you must be ready to deal with stress both from those higher up and those immediately below you. For skilled tradesmen and laborers, the pressures of finishing jobs on time, or even rushing to complete projects that have been delayed through no fault of their own, can be equally aggravating.

Jobs in Construction: A Rundown

One more useful way to examine construction is to divide up the various jobs that comprise it. Workers in some positions—some requiring years of training and experience—may be required on many different kinds of projects. A majority of

Sometimes extreme weather—including long hours in the hot sun, or sometimes very cold conditions when a job has to be done on time—are one aspect of construction work that all laborers (and many contractors) should be ready for.

construction work requires a high school diploma or passing a General Educational Development test, commonly known as a GED.

Workers in specialized skilled trades sometimes take courses to be certified in a specialty, which can be done at

A man lays brick in Boston, Massachusetts. Many construction jobs require skill and an attention to detail while being able to do the same tasks over and over again. Being proud of good workmanship is one plus of construction work.

technical schools, either before or while they gain work experience. Others learn on the job, many of these also gaining skills and experience via apprenticeships, which are explained later. Taking a look at a few of the jobs and the personal characteristics suitable for each can give readers an idea of where they might fit in within the construction industry.

Laborer

Perhaps the most common of all construction jobs someone can get is that of laborer. It is the one that requires the least skills, but considerable amounts of work, nonetheless. They are likely to do the most physically demanding tasks, and will often work at great heights or outside in sometimes tough weather conditions, including hot and cold weather.

Laborers are required on every job, large or small, and usually in every aspect of a job. They need to be jacks (or jills) of all trades, train on the job, and quickly be able to learn any of the simpler tasks required of them. In some cases, they may help different crews on different days or stages of a project.

It helps to have some kind of experience, but some jobs may hire without it, especially if more senior workers and supervisors are hiring friends or acquaintances for very basic tasks (one reason word of mouth and networking count so much in construction). This again underscores that learning fast, working hard, and having stamina and physical ability are the main prerequisites of the job. The ability to follow directions and not chafe under authority is also key.

Masons

Masons build, repair, and maintain concrete walls and fences, chimneys, terraces, stone and concrete floors, patios, fireplaces, and other stone and brick structures. Masonry refers to building anything that combines various materials with mortar, a mixed paste combining cement, water, and sand.

Brick masons, also known as bricklayers, build with bricks and mortar. Stone masons use natural stone components to make things like walls, pillars, patios, and bridges, also using mortar and sometimes grout to set stones in place.

Another subset of masonry is tilesetting, in which tile is laid in bathrooms and kitchens and other spaces, including walls, floors, and ceilings.

Concrete masons, perhaps the most well known in this construction category, use poured concrete and concrete bricks to build a wide variety of things. Many concrete masons learn specialized tasks and processes, including creating concrete of specific textures, finishes, and colors.

Masons of all kinds should have physical strength and stamina, and be able to carry loads of more than fifty pounds, including heavy tools and equipment. They should have good hand-eye coordination, be able to recognize color and texture differences, have math skills to properly measure and mix materials, and have some sense of graphic design and aesthetics, when working on self-directed, smaller jobs.

Carpenters

Just as masons work with stone and brick, carpenters work primarily with wood and related materials to build the frameworks and interiors of walls, stairways, partitions, door frames and other structures that make up the skeletons of buildings. They

BUILDING: A TECH CAREER

While many people do not consider construction to be a high-tech field, modern building proves otherwise. Building structures was one of the first human-developed technologies, for starters.

From learning and mastering software that allows for reading and modifying blueprints, to using spreadsheets for materials cost analyses, to crafting a building schedule that works with budgets and payrolls, computer and digital technology is intimately tied into all facets of construction.

In the near and distant future, even laborers may be required to master new technologies that will save time and money. Many industry observers believe drones will be used to survey building sites and to examine and even help make repairs of building exteriors and hard-to-get-to places. 3D printing techniques will potentially help with new and innovative building plans, and may even be used to pour concrete and other materials.

In addition, green building technologies have also become among the newest and most important trend in modern construction. Designing and forming structures using sustainable practices and materials will ensure that current and future generations of construction workers will have to adapt to a green building future.

also make and install cabinets, work with drywall (used to create interior walls and ceilings), and oversee many other different parts of a job, including installing molding, windows, and fixtures.

Because of these varied tasks, carpenters are often the first workers on a project, and the last to work on it, too. They work both outdoors and indoors on many different jobs, including offices, houses, highway construction, and much more. Besides helping construct the buildings themselves, they also build scaffolding for their own use and that of other workers.

Many aspects of carpentry, including working in cramped spaces, are physically demanding. Carpenters must constantly switch positions, whether they are standing, kneeling, lifting, or even crawling, and they often deal with the highest injury rates in the industry. While rare, they must beware of potentially fatal falls, and getting cut by tools and sharp surfaces.

Overall, carpenters should be physically flexible and agile, have physical strength and stamina, be very detail oriented, skilled in math, and good at problem solving. They need varied skills because they potentially oversee many project details.

Ironworkers

Ironworkers—like their wood-loving counterparts, carpenters—install iron and steel to create frameworks for buildings, bridges, roads, and other structures and spaces. This dangerous and physically demanding work requries wearing safety harnesses while high up in the air. Ironworking may involve:

- reinforcing steel and cable in concrete structures (called rebar work);
- erecting the metal skeletons of buildings;

- installing window wall and curtain wall exteriors;
- working the rigging (cables, pullies, winches, and other tools) and cranes to move and raise heavy equipment up to where it is needed;
- welding—joining together pieces or parts of metal together using heating tools like blowtorches or electric arcs, and pressing and hammering them together.

Carpentry is one of the most popular and lucrative jobs in the construction industry. There are few phases of a building project in which carpenters do not contribute.

Pipefitters, Steamfitters, and Plumbers

The pipes that carry water, fuel, sewage, and other gases and materials in and out of buildings are crucial to keep any business, institution, or home running smoothly. The ones who install and repair these are known as pipefitters, steamfitters, and plumbers. These include not just the pipes in bathrooms and kitchens, but the ones that run through buildings and feed into sewers or septic systems.

As their name implies, pipefitters fit pipes into piping systems. They install and assemble pipes, make repairs, and often fabricate them, too; that is, they cut, bend, and reshape pipes to fit and join them in particular ways, by welding and sometimes using chemical methods. In smaller jobs, one or two pipefitters may be enough. In larger buildings, very large pipes need a crew of people to help lift and fit them.

Plumbers perform similar work, but they are employed far more in residential construction, along with some commercial enterprises, like small businesses. Pipefitters handle more industrial-scale work. While plumbers deal mainly with water and sewage piping, pipefitters employ different materials for a wider variety of gases, steam, chemicals, and other hazardous materials. Steamfitters are similar to pipefitters—and in some regions, they are interchangeable—but are more likely to work with high-pressure liquids and gases. Both also install and maintain automatic controls and gauges that regulate what goes through the pipes.

Electricians

Nearly every part of the built landscape needs power feeding it somehow, making electricians indispensible to the construction field. They install, help maintain, and repair the wiring, circuitry, and other equipment used to keep buildings and other places on the grid. This includes conduits and tubes that carry wiring. They are vital to making sure its inhabitants have lighting, Internet access, security, power to run machines, appliances, and computers, and, in many cases, running water, heating, and other systems.

Electricians must be extremely detail oriented, and have strength and stamina, excellent hand-to-eye coordination, and preferably some exposure to science and math in their education. Their job is particularly dangerous because shoddy work, or even a single mistake can expose them and others to electrocution or fire-related hazards.

Heavy Equipment Operators

For young children, this is likely the job most identified with the words "construction worker." As fun as it looked (or may still look), this job is far from child's play. The serious business of running bulldozers, cranes, excavators, loaders, and backhoes takes skill, strength, and precision. These machines are used mainly to dig out and move earth, and sometimes in demolition.

Other machines used in construction include cement mixers, and specialized equipment made for building highways, such as drills, chip spreaders, cold planers, compactors, graders, pavers, and more. Operators of these big machines need to be physically fit, careful, and well trained. The stakes are very high because nearly every moving vehicle employed on work sites can easily cause fatal accidents if mishandled.

Demolition

Demolition is one of the more dangerous and intensive jobs you can get in construction. Higher-skilled workers in this sector demolish buildings using heavy equipment like cranes and wrecking balls, bulldozers, or other machines. Larger buildings, such as big office towers, can be demolished with explosives, such as dynamite.

A construction manager gives instructions to a heavy equipment operator. Safety and precision are important qualities to uphold for workers who operate such useful and powerful machinery.

One of the more popular options these days is stripping buildings out manually, in which lesser-skilled workers take apart buildings floor by floor, even with hand tools. This is done to salvage (or save) many of the still usable materials and infrastructure, like wire, pipes, and even wood, concrete, brick, and metal. For obvious reasons—especially falling and collapsing materials—this is one of the most dangerous construction subsectors.

Specialization

There are many other positions in construction, especially in specialized fields, and others in managerial and supervisory positions, which we will cover shortly. It is important to remember that, besides laborers, most construction workers who hope to rise in the ranks will pick a skill and work on it. Higher up the ladder, only certain jobs require someone to work with a variety of teams or crews on the job, and hence require more generalized knowledge. Even skilled tradespeople benefit from knowing how the big picture ties together, however.

An Educational Foundation

The road to landing a job in construction can start very early for someone who is handy. Boys, and increasingly girls, who are good with their hands usually know by the time they are in junior high school or thereabouts that they enjoy and are good at it. There is no time like the present, and there are ways to develop such talents both in and out of school. Much like construction workers build a home from the ground up, the path to working in this industry can begin with a solid foundation.

Talking Shop

While they have disappeared from many schools in recent years, if you are lucky enough to attend a school with shop classes, it is advised that you take as many as you can. The two main, "classic" shop classes have been wood shop and metal shop, giving pupils good introductions to carpentry and metalworking. Teachers start students with the basics—learning how to use basic hand and power tools safely, to selecting wood and metal for simple projects, and then planning out and completing them. Students in wood shop can learn to make items such as birdhouses, stools, shelves, clocks, boxes, and more. In metal shop, they can try their hand at producing common tools like bottle openers, screwdrivers, letter openers, hammers, as well as paperweights, metal stamps, and other useful items.

As more schools begin to concentrate on Science, Technology, Engineering, and Math (STEM) education, many educators and shop teachers hope that schools will return to these classic and productive classes.

Technical High Schools

If you have made up your mind early on to concentrate on the manual arts (as some people call mechanical skills), and are lucky enough to live in an area which offers them, you can apply to a technical high school, sometimes known as a vocational-technical (or vo-tech) high school. Some school districts call this career and technical education (CTE). They may even cooperate with community colleges in your area to offer classes to qualified high school seniors.

Other Useful Subjects

There is an unfortunately common myth that handy and mechanically inclined students do not need or can slack off when it comes to their academic subjects. However, excelling in English, mathematics, physics, and other classes can only help you in your career and personal development if you enter the construction industry. Being able to communicate well, both orally and using the written word, is essential to doing construction work well, making English class particularly valuable. Mathematics will sharpen your mind and analytical abilities, and prepare you for the many calculations to be made on all work sites.

Physics, chemistry, and engineering classes provide the background on how materials interact, and how architectural

A high school wood shop instructor, shown second from left, looks on with the rest of the class as one of his students cuts a piece of wood. Shop class is a fantastic opportunity to find out if you have what it takes to work in construction.

planning and construction engineering determine efficient and safe building practices. Future electricians, carpenters, plumbers, and many other construction workers and contractors will always benefit from well-rounded course selection early on.

Other classes that can be useful down the line for future construction workers, if they are available, include mechanical and computer drafting, 3D printing, typing and business courses, and automotive repair.

Visiting a Counselor

You may be very confident that you will pursue a construction career, or you may have some questions. However confident or informed you think you are, a great idea is to visit your high school guidance or career counselor. If you are truly ahead of the curve, even a junior high or middle school counselor may be able to help you, especially if your district offers students placement in special technical high schools or similar programs in regular ones.

A guidance counselor will review your classes and academic progress and give you pointers on which ones, particularly electives, will best prepare you for later technical training. Counselors have knowledge about what programs are out there, what partnerships your school may have with other schools and institutions and businesses, and if any extracurricular activities the school and its community offer can be helpful. By showing interest, you may also find out about scholarships and internships and apprenticeships that could help, too. Your counselor will know to give you tips on these opportunities when he or she gets word of them.

Taking College Classes in High School

One of the potential benefits of asking early (and often) about specialized technical training in high school is getting in on the ground floor by voicing your interest in adult-level classes. Your best bet to be placed in such classes is to show promise in your other coursework, so make sure to keep your grades up. Then you can apply to programs in which you either take technical classes that count toward college credit in your own school, or you can travel off campus to a community college, four-year college, or a technical school.

Many vocational high schools specialize in such placement, and even traditional ones can help you sign up for them. Some of the types of classes you can take for transferable credits give you hands-on experience in some basic skills many construction careers require. These include training in the use of

Chemistry and other science classes can help you learn about the natural world and especially about the material properties of matter. This knowledge is highly useful later in the hands-on environment of building.

A guidance counselor will be able to answer many of the questions you may have about which classes to take and what schools to apply to if you are set on pursuing a career in construction.

hand and power tools, reading and interpreting blueprints and technical manuals, and becoming familiar with more complex machinery. Many current programs not only expose students to new and modern equipment, but also are up to date with the newest techniques in environmentally sustainable construction practices, also known as "green building" construction.

Vocational and Trade Schools

Whether you are able to take advantage of such programs or not, the next stage in your education might be entering the job market directly. However, for those workers who want to learn a skilled trade (versus paying their dues only as a general construction laborer), the best option is to take your education to the next level. Going to college or university to pursue academics is not for everyone. Young people who are drawn to the construction industry may opt instead to attend a vocational school, also known as a trade school.

Trade schools do not require mastery in academic subjects, but instead concentrate on the core training each student needs for a particular skilled trade or industry sector they apply to learn about. Students can select whether they will specialize in a particular trade, or take coursework that provides an overview of skills needed for construction.

A construction manager makes a phone call while going over some paperwork. Managers and other supervisory personnel must be savvy in the building trades and prove capable as administrators.

TRAINING FOR MANAGEMENT: CONTRACTORS, CMS, AND ESTIMATORS

Other important jobs in construction are managerial ones. Smaller, independent companies—and the individuals that run them—are known as contractors. A contractor may specialize in a particular trade, such as carpentry or demolition. Small projects may include a single contractor who hires a variety of skilled tradespeople, or may even employ several contractors working together on a single site, whether a house, business, or other project.

In bigger companies, managerial positions that are in charge of whole work sites, or smaller jobs that make up very big ones, are held by construction managers (shortened to CM in many cases), or project managers. As construction techniques become ever more sophisticated, many companies are increasingly requiring candidates for CM and other managerial positions to have completed some form of formal education.

Another important managerial job in construction is that of an estimator. Estimators and chief estimators make and track bids for work. A contractor trying to get another company's business will place a bid, which estimates the amount of money the former will do a particular job for. Often, two or more contractors will bid to work on a job, and the one who offers to do it the cheapest and quickest wins out, as long as his or her client finds the offer and plan credible. Along with handling the bidding game, estimators negotiate budgets, read and interpret construction plans to calculate possible costs, manage the estimating team, and track and analyze data to make sure they are accurate.

Promising candidates for such managerial posts are sometimes picked from a company's general ranks and sent to school, if their employers feel like investing in someone long-term. Otherwise, many younger employees opt to finish a two-year associate's degree at a community college, called an Associate of Science, or AS degree, in construction management, construction science, or building science. Many community colleges and private schools now even offer bachelor's and even master's degrees in construction and project management. Students in all of these programs learn about safety codes and building standards, project management, project design, construction methods and materials management, and how to estimate costs.

Other leadership roles on job sites may be drawn from rank-and-file workers, and include job titles such as foreman, crew leader, lead hand, and superintendent, among others. These are discussed in a bit more detail in a separate section.

Trade schools tailor their course offerings to allow those who already have jobs (whether in construction or otherwise) to study evenings, weekends, and during summers, too. The length of programs often varies, but many programs can be completed in a year or less.

For example, one chain of trade schools in Maryland called North American Trade Schools, which currently has a good rating with the state's Better Business Bureau, advertises that it offers thirty-nine-week courses in building construction or electrical technology. Its construction program covers carpentry, roofing, interior framing, and millwork (a type of decorative and functional woodworking).

There is probably a school somewhere within commuting and/or driving distance from you that fits your needs, and offers courses as specific or as general as you feel you will need when first entering the construction field. Get online, ask your guidance counselor, and ask family members, friends, and anyone else you can to find out more.

Applying for Financial Aid

Just as many college and university students rely on federally administered student loans to attend two- and four-year colleges, such loans are also available to applicants of programs in skilled trades, whether offered via community colleges or private trade schools. Any reputable school will have an admissions and financial aid office willing to provide information on and arrange a meeting about loans and other assistance that students of any income levels can apply for.

Make sure to look online to thoroughly research any school you are thinking of attending, to check their reputation. If you have anyone in your social circle—on social media, or elsewhere—who has attended a trade school, ask them about it. Be careful and never sign any paperwork for loans, or turn over any payments, until you have read what you are paying for.

If necessary, have an adult or other knowledgeable party (even a lawyer or other financial adviser) check it out for you. The biggest dangers include being targeted in an outright scam, or being fooled into attending "diploma mills"—that is, schools that make big promises about coursework, state-of-the-art equipment, and incredible job placement after you graduate, only to fall short or completely fail at meeting these promises. Pick wisely, and you will not regret it when you finally learn valuable skills in the trade school of your choice.

CHAPTER THREE

Trade Schools and Apprenticeships

Your progress in the construction industry depends on how, exactly, you enter it. As discussed, many workers enter the industry at the ground floor, as construction laborers. This is especially true for those who either cannot afford to defer earning money while attending school, or cannot afford school, even with loans, a fact of life for many young people nowadays. Others do not want to incur a substantial financial debt.

However, a good career in construction can help someone pay off their student debt relatively quickly compared to holders of bachelor's degree, since, according to numbers on 2013 from the National Center for Education Statistics, the average trade school degree or certificate will run about $33,000, versus about $127,000 for a four-year institution. It is a good option for someone who has a very good idea about the kind of construction work they want to do. Those who are unsure and want to sample the terrain may opt instead to find general work and decide on the job.

Coursework in Trade Schools

There are no exact or universal standards for coursework that trade schools need to provide in any of the construction disciplines. General courses—in which someone learns a bit about everything, and "majors" in a particular skill—are often called "construction trades" by many schools nationwide. Other schools may have formal training for a year (and sometimes longer) that exposes students to far greater specialization.

For example, a trade school certificate in carpentry will initially focus on fundamentals, such as tools, materials, and using ladders and other equipment. Other topics include

Beginning to learn your skills in a school geared toward teaching the trades is a good option for many reasons. Trade schools for general construction skills and for specialized trades exist in nearly every city and county.

It is the opportunity to learn directly from experienced instructors that makes trade school a good choice for those who want to enter the construction workforce with already developed skills, whether in carpentry or other trades.

reading blueprints, framing (building structural frameworks), and learning building codes. Hands-on instruction usually follows, with topics such as building foundations, building and finishing floors, walls and ceilings, putting in roofing, exterior finishing, insulation and ventilation techniques, doors, stair framing and stairs, and building cabinets.

Many schools let students pick and explore specializations alongside their general coursework. Later, when looking for work, they can pick different jobs that fall under general carpentry, such as millwright, floor layers, drywall applicator, lathe specialist, pile driver, and many other specializations.

Theoretical and Hands-On Instruction

Trade school programs (and similar community college courses in the trades) often offer a basic foundation in theoretical instruction, conducted via reading technical texts and attending classroom lectures. These will usually cover federal and state safety requirements, often before students are given hands-on training.

Hands-on teaching and doing is the bread and butter of trade school coursework, and is what students really pay for: skilled practitioners guiding novices in the basics, and gradually helping them build up their skills.

Paying attention and taking all of the lessons of trade school coursework to heart is important, because in construction there is no room for error. Cutting corners or making careless mistakes can harm you, your coworkers and superiors, and innocent strangers who later inhabit or frequent buildings you work on, both on the job site, and even much later.

Getting an Apprenticeship

Many trade schools have partnerships with potential employers in their particular town, city, and/or region, and often offer job placement services, which are among the biggest attractions for students who attend them.

Job placement may or may not include apprenticeship training programs. For those with little real earlier experience (for example, as a construction laborer), these can be a great opportunity. A larger trade school may provide as many types of apprenticeship as it has programs of coursework, in jobs as diverse as electrician, glazier (glass worker), carpet and tile laying, ironworking, carpentry, bricklaying, and many more. Smaller schools with more specialized programs will naturally concentrate on more targeted apprenticeships.

MASONRY: STONE AND CONCRETE AND SCHOOLWORK

To provide an example of the type of schooling a trade school student might experience, consider a typical course load that provides someone with an entry-level understanding of masonry. Some masonry instruction schools can run as long as two years because of the high level of skill needed for this particular career choice.

Consequently, masons are among the highest paid of the skilled tradesmen in construction. Certificate and diploma programs, which are shorter, provide more basic instruction, while associate degree programs may add on business and management courses that prepare masons for higher-level managerial jobs as supervisors, managers, or as contractor-owners of masonry and bricklaying companies.

Introductory courses teach student masons about the concepts behind working with stone, concrete, and making blocks and bricks. They are introduced to tools such as levels, jointers, trowels, and machinery, and are instructed on how to mix and spread mortar. Early lessons include how to keep construction sites safe, and how to avoid injury around tools and equipment.

Further coursework delves into how to read blueprints and build structures based on them. Students learn how to translate the drawings, symbols, and terminology on schematics into real-life brick and stone components and structures. Learning building codes, at least on a general level, is also a requirement.

Hands-on instruction usually follows, and often begins with bricklaying small structures in class. Straight brick walls are the first project, followed by steps, door jambs, corners, and fireplace surrounds.

Once students have been exposed to and mastered the basics, they learn advanced brick masonry and design. In this course, they learn how to construct chimneys and residential building arches, and other more advanced structures made of ornamental brick.

Other specializations for masons, especially popular in recent years, have included courses in which students learn to repair and maintain historic masonry, whether on classic homes or on structures that have been classified historic landmarks. Historic preservation has made this an in-demand skill, which requires understanding of how such buildings were originally constructed, and aesthetically recreating the feel and look of old buildings.

Apprentices, Masters, and Journeymen

By definition, apprenticeship refers to a working and mentoring relationship in which the novice or inexperienced newcomer works under the supervision of an experienced, usually older member of his or her trade. Apprenticeships vary widely in length, and regulations on how long are irregular throughout the United States. On average, they last between one and six years, depending on the trade.

Take, for instance, the road an electrician travels, beginning with an apprenticeship. According to the Department of Labor (DOL), most such apprenticeships last about four years. During this time, the apprentice works closely under their more experienced mentor. When the apprenticeship is over, the electrician is now considered a journeyman, and can work without supervision, but usually still with some guidance.

The worker then spends about three to six years being a journeyman electrician. They install wiring, outlets, and fixtures, do service work, and troubleshoot power failures. They typically do not secure work permits on their own, but work under permits issued to those higher up: master electricians.

Before he or she moves to the next level, a journeyman usually studies more electricity fundamentals, managing

The master and apprentice relationship is similar to having a dedicated teacher in high school or trade school, but is often more personalized. Working closely on the job with an expert in your trade is the way most novices rise in the industry.

Young apprentices benefit from thoughtful and supportive mentors. Unlike some jobs in the service economy and even the white collar world, age and experience are a plus in the skilled trades.

projects, safety rules and regulations, and building codes. This may require classes for certification at either a school or an industry-approved training program, and passing a test. The journeyman then becomes a master electrician.

Masters are the ones who directly supervise apprentices, and who journeymen answer turn to for guidance and leadership when needed. They also decide what kinds of wiring to use and other major decisions on jobs of all sizes.

Registered Apprenticeships

Registered apprenticeship programs differ from on-the-job apprenticeships because they are conducted along with a minimum set of hours of classroom instruction. They have been common in the skilled trades for decades, and most require that someone apply for them, and be at least eighteen years of age. Some require a trade school certificate or diploma in a particular trade already, while most do not.

They are often administered by professional organizations, such as a state association made up of many different construction firms, for example. Many unions also provide such apprenticeships for novice workers. Some require union membership to take advantage, but others are open to anyone. Employers of all kinds, community college and state college systems, industry associations, and even the military sponsor and help administer registered apprenticeships.

It is in the interests of both businesses and unions that skilled workers continue to be trained and deployed to the state and national workforces. Many skilled construction trades have experienced a shortage of necessary workers in recent years, especially as older blue-collar workers retire or otherwise leave the labor market.

APPRENTICESHIPS FOR DIFFERENT SKILLED TRADES

According to the U.S. Bureau of Labor Statistics (BLS), there are a few main occupational categories in construction in which apprenticeship is a common entry point for workers: stonemasons; brickmasons and blockmasons; carpenters; electricians; glaziers; mechanical insulation workers; plumbers, pipefitters, and steamfitters; iron and rebar workers; sheet metal workers; structural iron and steel workers; and Terrazzo workers and finishers.

Here are some figures estimating averages, and how long apprenticeships take for a sampling of construction trades.

Carpenter	4 years
Electricians	4 years
Plumbers	3-4 years
Welders	3 years
Bricklayers	3 years
Roofers	3 years
Pipefitters	4-5 years

This arrangement, known typically as "Earn and Learn," was taken advantage of by about 130,000 workers who entered an apprenticeship in 2011, according to the U.S. Department of Labor's Bureau of Labor Statistics (BLS). That same year, about 55,000 individuals completed a registered apprenticeship.

The BLS also estimates that applicants who complete registered apprenticeships earn an average of about $300,000 during the course of their career versus those in the same jobs who do not. They typically start at about $15 an hour working, and participate in a program that has high national and state standards for instruction.

While some have a minimum age of sixteen years to apply, most individuals must be eighteen years old in jobs that count as hazardous occupations, which most construction is classified as. Some of the most popular construction jobs with registered apprenticeships include carpentry, electrician, pipefitters, and more. Being selected to this kind of apprenticeship is determined by the sponsoring organization, and may require minimum grades in high school, taking particular aptitude tests, and personal interviews. One huge benefit is that participants start earning right away. Completing such an apprenticeship leaves a well-trained worker with little or no student debt.

Working as a journeyman (like this electrician, for example) represents the middle tier of experience, prestige, and earning power in the construction industry. With patience, steady work, and applying onself, being a master is not far off.

CHAPTER FOUR

What Jobs Are Out There and How to Get Them

Whether you are entering the job market cold or seeking work with the help of a trade school's job placement program, or via an apprenticeship, many job search techniques can work for you. These include getting your resume out there, looking for work in a variety of ways, and some basics on interviewing.

Getting Your Resume Out There

When you are first starting out, your resume should be short and to the point, and list your work experience, starting with most recent and current positions first, with earlier experience listed later. It should detail your technical skills, relevant certifications and internships, and relevant accomplishments (volunteering to help build a house, for example).

To get your resume format right, consult the Internet, a guidance counselor in high school, a job placement specialist at a trade school, or even a trusted adult—one working in construction could be particularly helpful.

Online Employment Sites

Once you have it finalized, it is time to get your resume out there. One way is to upload it and search around on as many general employment websites as you can. These include EmploymentGuide.com, CareerBuilder, Monster.com, Indeed.com, Simply Hired, Snagajob, and JobBankUSA.

Checking out Monster.com and other job sites is one part of a multifaceted job search. For entry-level workers, such sites will be even more valuable, until they start developing industry contacts, especially before landing an apprenticeship.

Geographic searches (using your zipcode, town, city, etc.), coupled with keyword searches for a specific job title ("roofer," "carpenter," "stonemason") should yield the best results. You can also set parameters for desired salary, benefits, and other variables.

You can respond to individual ads, as well as upload your resume on particular sites, and set up automatic delivery when specific jobs are listed, or receive automatic e-mail alerts whenever such jobs appear on them. Most sites will require or encourage you to set up a user profile that uses much of your resume's information.

If you lack Internet service at home or via a mobile device, your school library, employment center at a trade school, or your local library may be options to get online for the job search. Your state department of labor or employment should have career resource centers available to the general public free of charge.

Extra Legwork and Word of Mouth

Don't limit your job search to general employment sites. Visit the web presences of individual companies in the building trades, real estate management companies, and government websites, to explore their job opportunities, too. Many trade magazines geared toward specific trades in construction have their own websites boasting editorial content, and often links to employment opportunities, too.

You should send e-mails and call companies hiring in your particular trade or sector even if they are not currently officially hiring. When they do so later, yours might already be in

Working on different job sites, you will work alongside people at all levels of experience in the industry. Do a good job, and you are more likely to be recommended by coworkers when others are hiring or putting work crews together.

their files. A hiring manager or other person higher up may remember your initiative. While being polite and not too pushy, do not hesitate to follow up every month or two to inquire if anything has opened up. Another idea is to physically show up at companies where you would like to work and drop off your resume. Keep it brief when you do so, and call ahead when possible. Some firms might welcome drop-ins, but many are wary of having people come in without official appointments.

Many unions specializing in construction trades advertise jobs, too, even if a majority of these require union membership to get them, though not all do. For certain jobs, union membership might be the smartest way to go. Examples of unions that offer apprenticeships and job opportunities include the International Brotherhood of Electrical Workers (IBEW), The International Union of Painters and Allied Trades (IUPAT), and the Laborers' International Union of North America (LIUNA), among many others.

Another popular and often fruitful path to get jobs in construction is by word of mouth. Establish networks and friendships with your fellow trade school students, coworkers on jobs you may have early on (during high school, for example), and chances are you will hear about people hiring before you see online ads for such jobs.

Many, if not most, employers prefer to take the recommendations of trusted coworkers or employees ahead of applicants who are strangers to them. They will especially do so when they get dozens and even hundreds of resumes for for a few openings. Never be afraid to mention to others that you are looking for work, or to put in a good word for you with someone they know. If you do land a job this way, be considerate and help someone else down the line in the same position. It is not just smart, but the right thing to do.

Interviewing: Doing It Right

The moment of truth arrives: you get a call back! The lead-up to actually interviewing for a position (especially one you really want) can be an exciting and nerve-racking time. There are many things to consider and plan for.

One thing to carefully consider is if the job you are interviewing is right for you. It is okay to try and go for positions that are perhaps ambitious, but think it through before you accept an appointment. A job listing or description may make it clear that they will not consider applicants without certain skills, accreditations, or experience. The absolute worst thing to do is fudge the facts or exaggerate on your resume. An experienced construction manager or other interviewer will see through such charades.

This is true for any job sector, but especially so for construction, where precision and high standards not only assure good work, but guarantee the safety of coworkers and others. Getting in over your head and ending up underqualified on a job site can waste your time, your boss's, and end up harming others.

The Day Of: Be Ready

Make sure to have a few copies of your resume printed out and on hand. While the interviewer likely has a printed copy of your e-mailed version, it shows initiative and preparedness. Another employee of the company may be brought in to evaluate or speak with you, and you want to be able to provide them with a copy as well.

Dress the Part

Use common sense when selecting your wardrobe for job interviews. The recent and popular advice given jobseekers— "Dress for the Job You Want"—applies to the construction field, too. There are white-collar positions in construction, especially on the business side of things that happen mostly in offices. For jobs like these, the best option actually is a nice business suit and polished shoes, for men and women (though women have the option to wear business slacks or a suit with skirt). This is also advisable if you are applying for a lower-level, hands-on construction job but hoping to climb the ladder into management or other white-collar work.

Mostly, however, construction is a blue-collar field. Workers wear casual and comfortable clothing for everyday work—clothing like jeans, flannel work shirts, sweatshirts, steel-toe boots for protection, warm and heavy coats for outdoor work, and similar gear. The wardrobe standard for employees interviewing for construction might be called smart casual, and business casual is also acceptable.

Dress neatly, in freshly laundered clothes that are not ripped or worn. A polo-style or golf shirt and khakis is acceptable. A sports jacket is fine instead of a two- or three-piece suit, as is a collared shirt with a sweater over it and slacks. Women can wear a sweater and slacks, too. Some interviewees even wear jeans (a smart casual touch), as long as this is offset by a blazer and shoes and a neat button-down shirt.

If you don't own the right clothes, consider borrowing from friends or family members. Given enough time,

Unless they are aiming for a white-collar office job in construction, most job seekers in the industry should dress neatly but appropriately. A smart casual look like this one is perfectly presentable and acceptable.

investigate sales at clothing shops and department stores, or, if on a really tight budget, try Goodwill, Salvation Army, and other thrift stores. It may take extra time, but with some effort, you can find something acceptable.

You do not want to go too casual, however. This includes wearing too little—such as sleeveless blouses or dresses for women, or even sleeveless shirts for men, even if you have seen construction workers in the hot sun on a worksite in summertime doing just that.

It is better to show up in a sober, neutral suit and look a little more dressed up than in beat-up sneakers and

GETTING THERE

One factor that can derail your prospects is some unforeseen problem on the way to the actual site of your interview. If you have more than a day or two before the interview, do a trial run, getting there at the appointed time, whether you are driving, being driven, taking a taxi or car service, or taking public transportation. Time yourself and then add another half hour to that time—the total should be your estimated commute. A flat tire, mechanical trouble, or unexpected bad weather can all slow you down or ruin your plans entirely. Figure out a plan B, and even a Plan C, giving yourself enough time to go a different way and make it on time. Ideally, you would like to be early, by about fifteen minutes.

When interviewing for a more office-oriented or non-hands-on positions, your interview may take place at a company's offices. This location is usually straightforward and easily determined, found via a plainly marked street address. But sometimes job interviews might be conducted in trailers on work sites, and it may not be readily apparent. where to go. You may need to walk around a bit or look more closely to figure out how to even enter a work site. Be careful and makes sure not to jump the gun and enter a secure area where you may accidentally hurt yourself, or get hurt because you are entering a construction site without a hard hat or other protective gear.

paint-spattered jeans and scuffed-up work boots. The latter just shows you are not serious and could even be interpreted as insulting.

In addition, while they are more socially acceptable than ever before, especially in blue-collar work, tattoos and piercings are still not universally accepted, and it is best to cover them up and/or remove them.

What You Will Talk About

While it seems that the employers have all the power (after all, you may need them more than they need you, specifically), think of interviewing as a two-way street. It can reduce your anxiety and tension about getting a new job, too. You are figuring out if the job is the right thing for you, just as the employers are determining your suitability for the work and the specific workplace.

Your interviewer may be a human resources person if it is a larger company, a manager or foreman in a construction crew, and sometimes even the owner/operator or contractor if it is a small company. He or she will want to know your experience, credentials, applicable apprenticeships, and other information in detail beyond what you included in your resume. Be prepared to talk at length about these things, and about what you hope to get out of the job besides a paycheck.

Some employers may have written tests to pass that demonstrate your familiarity with building trades concepts or processes, or may even require skills testing on a job site. Others will take your word for it, based upon your credentials. Be prepared to back up what you claim. As discussed earlier, exaggerating your skills or qualifications is always a

A positive attitude and confidence during an interview should always work in your favor, but make sure not to come off cocky or arrogant. A smile and a firm handshake and good eye contact, are key as well.

mistake; you will be exposed sooner or later. Do not squander the goodwill of potential employers and risk your working reputation.

Rolling with the Punches

You may be hired on the spot, or told that you will hear back soon. It does not hurt to call soon to check on the status of your application or hiring. Definitely e-mail or otherwise send a thank-you note to everyone you met during your interview and visit. Some jobs require two or more phases of interviewing, and the further along you make it, the better chance you will get the position.

You may not hear back, or get bad news: you didn't get the job. Do not let it get you down or stress you out. The important thing is that you tried. Dust yourself off, send more resumes out, talk to more friends and acquaintances, and apply yourself. You will make it if you try, and land the job in construction you want and need.

CHAPTER FIVE

The First Day on the Job, and Beyond

You get the call back—the one that really counts: You're hired! Celebrate all you want. You have earned it. But this moment of triumph is only the beginning of your journey as you enter the construction field. There is much to learn, and getting used to the working world takes more than simply doing the tasks you were trained to do.

Getting Started

Your first days on the job will vary depending on the position. Office jobs in construction tend to concentrate more on paperwork, while new employees who are laborers or tradesmen will likely get started working hands-on right away. But everyone new on a job, especially in bigger organizations, usually has to fill out paperwork and fulfill other bureaucratic and administrative tasks the first day and week on the job.

For example, you may meet with someone in human resources, or a superior, to be presented a packet of paperwork to fill out, as well as paperwork to sign that declares you have read and accepted certain terms of employment. These include receipt of employee manuals that cover policies and procedures.

Such materials tell you in detail rules of behavior on the job, including guidelines on Internet usage, how to respectfully talk to and address both superiors and subordinates, policies on sexual harassment and workplace violence and conflict, and common restrictions, such as requiring zero tolerance policies on drug and alcohol consumption and abuse on the job. One part of the latter may be employee drug testing, which has become more common in recent decades.

Other paperwork you will fill out will be withholding forms for federal, state, and local taxes, as well as signing receipts of workmen's compensation policies and procedures—that is, if you are hurt on the job, and are unable to work, or require medical attention or even surgery or other health procedures. Workmen's comp often covers much or all of someone's bills in case of accidents, but the rules vary among the states and other jurisdictions. It is advisable that you study the rules to know your rights in case of injury.

The same is true when it comes to your employee health plan, if one is offered (it usually is). There is usually no rush when it comes to picking a plan—whether you receive instant coverage upon hiring, or if coverage only kicks in after a set period (say, three months), you usually have some time to select something that suits you.

If you obtained your job through a union, the union officer or representative at your company or on the job site may meet with you to discuss issues, questions, or procedures that your membership touches upon.

Make an effort to do your job well, and learn as much you can the first days, weeks, and months on a new job. One of your best resources is consulting older, more experienced workers, beyond simply master tradesmen and mentors.

Impress Them from the Beginning

You want to make a good first impression your first day, and the first week. Try to show up early if possible. Make sure you are prepared. If you are going to be handling tools and getting your hands dirty the first day, remember to dress the part, and bring all the gear you need, including any cold-weather protection if necessary. Employees might need to show up already dressed in their work gear on some jobs, while other ones have changing areas. Whatever the case, show up well rested and well groomed.

For those on a career track in the office or management ranks, make a note during your interview(s) what others are wearing, and dress accordingly. If it is unclear for any reason, do not be afraid to call and ask.

You may get your own cubicle, office, locker, or workstation. Make sure to keep any real estate assigned to you neat and orderly, because its condition reflects well or poorly on you. Management is watching, just as they are watching you carefully to see if you are learning quickly, applying yourself, and meeting and/or exceeding the standards in whatever tasks assigned and expected of you. A new hire needs to prove themselves, and keep doing so.

Keeping Things Professional

The paperwork you received, and possibly even some mandatory videos that are common throughout many industries, will detail the definitions of appropriate and inappropriate behavior when it comes to romantic involvement or entanglements on the job. Even among peers who are at the same level of employment, relationships, dating, and sexual contact are discouraged (especially on the job, but even after hours). This is because it is often difficult to determine who is

The modern construction site and workplace has come a long way in the last few decades. Diverse workplace mean that everyone should be mindful of the feelings and contributions of their fellow workers, regardless of background.

in the right if a situation deteriorates and spills and affects the daily working environment.

Relations are especially discouraged and frowned upon—and are often grounds for termination or other discipline—between bosses and underlings. Those who violate these rules put themselves in danger of getting fired or other sanctions, and bosses are especially discouraged from pursuing relationships with their employees. Sexual harassment or creating a hostile work environment are especially frowned upon and can result in serious repercussions.

Keep it Safe, Always

Because of the great potential for bodily harm and death on a work site, safety is usually priority number one. If you find that you

CHAIN OF COMMAND

Another area where discipline and strict rules are enforced in construction is in the hierarchy of managers, foremen, tradesmen, and laborers. The chain of command, while varying from company to company, and among job sites, is very specific because everyone is kept highly accountable for their work and tasks to the people above. Clear and proper hierarchy provides every worker with their expected roles and responsibilities, and helps buildings and other projects run on schedule—and safely. Keeping on-site workers safe in particular is one of the highest priorities. Someone who is constantly challenging his or her superiors on minor points, or questioning why particular safety measures are in place, should prepare themselves to make few friends on the job. Following reasonable orders quickly and to the letter is necessary to the smooth running of a construction site.

are hired on to work somewhere where safety rules are being regularly violated or ignored, do not hesitate to contact your union representative, a trusted superior, or someone from the Occupational Safety and Health Administration (OSHA). OSHA is part of the U.S. Department of Labor and governs workplace safety rules and standards in construction and other industry. OHSA is also shorthand for the wide body of regulations themselves.

Beyond the responsibilities of your employers and coworkers to adhere to OSHA and other rules, the onus is on you to stay sharp, dress properly and safely, and remain ever vigilant to make sure you are not injured or cause injury to others. Construction workers must always don their hard hats on a site, and other safety gear when necessary, such as protective equipment for welding, protective suits and/or masks for hazardous materials removal. Workers who work high up off the ground must secure themselves with straps and harnesses. Tools should be put away and stored safely, or set aside in the least dangerous way possible while they are unused. The same is true for building materials, whether hazardous or not.

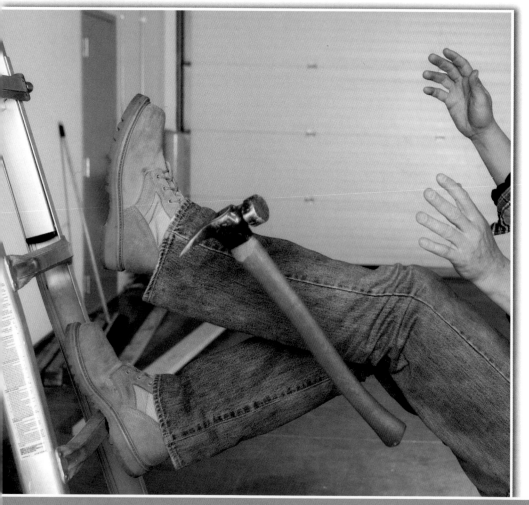

One of the greatest pitfalls of working in construction is accidental workplace injury. Knowing your rights and your employer's responsiblities to you is important. The ideal ways to deal with accidents are extreme caution and prevention.

Training and landing apprenticeships or entry-level work is just the beginning of a job in contruction. Get ready for a sometimes physically demanding but dynamic career that's hands-on, vital, and well paid.

A Tough but Rewarding Career

A career in construction can be stressful—tough on the body and mind alike. But it is also one filled with accomplishment and pride, despite the aches and pains one may suffer. It is considered a "recession-proof" career.

While periodic down-turns (such as the 2008 housing crash that slowed down new construction) will always occur, people will always need to build things, all around the world, including homes, businesses, institutions, public gathering and sports facilities, and many other kinds of projects. If you have the determination and skills, roll up your sleeves, because you will not regret working toward a job in the construction industry.

GLOSSARY

apprentice A person who learns a construction trade by working directly under a more experienced tradesman.

business casual Refers to a wardrobe style slightly less formal than a traditional business suit.

construction manager A person who manages the many different people on a work site or project, and many different aspects from scheduling to safety.

contractor An independent businessperson who is hired to organize building a house, building, or other construction project.

diploma mill A private trade or technical school that provides substandard or poor instruction and job placement services, and exists mainly to generate profit at the expense of educating its students.

foreman The leader of a construction crew, or group of workers belonging to the same trade.

journeyman A tradesman who has moved on from an apprenticeship to become a skilled worker in his or her own right.

glazier A construction tradesman who is in charge of cutting and installing glass.

G.E.D. Stands for General Educational Development, and refers to the test one takes as a substitute or equivalent for a high school diploma when applying to school or to the job market.

manual arts Another word for skills that involve working hands-on, with tools and technical know-how.

master A tradesman who has earned the necessary credentials and graduated from journeyman status.

STEM Short for Science, Technology, Engineering, and Math is a modern term for schools concentrating resources on subjects considered more technical than the humanities.

union An organization of workers in the same job sector, trade, or industry that team together to bargain with management for wages, benefits, and work rules and conditions favorable to its membership.

vocational-technical Sometimes known as "vo-tech," or simply vocational, refers to educational institutions that prepare students for a particular job or career, especially in a trade.

American Institute of Constructors
700 North Fairfax Street, Suite 510
Alexandria, VA 22314
(703) 683-4999
Website: http://professionalconstructor.site-ym.com
The American Institute of Constructors is a trade organization establishing standards of quality for the construction
industry, in addition to providing education and
certifications.

Canadian Apprenticeship Forum
404-2197 Riverside Drive
Ottawa, ON K1H 7X3
Canada
(613) 235-4004
Website: http://caf-fca.org
The Canadian Apprenticeshiip Forum is a nonprofit organization promoting apprenticeship throughout Canada's
provinces, including the Careers in Trade program target-
ing the building trades.

International Brotherhood of Electrical Workers (IBEW)
1125 15th Street NW
Washington, DC 20005
(202) 728-9033
Website: http://www.ibew.org
The International Brotherhood of Electrical Workers is a
labor union representing about 750,000 electricians and
workers in related trades and jobs.

Occupational Safety & Health Administration (OSHA)
200 Constitution Avenue NW
Washington, DC 20210
(800) 321-OSHA (6742)
Website: http://www.osha.gov
OSHA is an agency in the U.S. Department of Labor that
works to standardize and maintain safety rules and
regulations surrounding the workplace, including on job
sites and within companies in the construction trades.

U.S. Department of Labor
Frances Perkins Building
200 Constitution Avenue NW
Washington DC 20210
(866) 4-USA-DOL (866-487-2365)
Website: http://www.dog.gov
The Department of Labor is in charge of labor policy for
the federal government, including setting standards,
tracking important employment statistics, and promoting
employee support in many sectors.

Websites

Because of the changing number of Internet links, Rosen
Publishing has developed an online list of websites related to
the subject of this book. This site is updated regularly. Please
use this link to access this list:

http://www.rosenlinks.com/JOBS/constr

FOR FURTHER READING

Beco, Alice. *Cool Careers Without College for People Who Love Houses*. Rosen Publishing, 2007.

Byers, Ann. *A Career as a Construction Manager* (Essential Careers). New York, NY: Rosen Publishing, 2016.

Byers, Ann. *Jobs as Green Builders and Planners*. New York, NY: Rosen Publishing, 2010.

Construction (Ferguson's Careers in Focus). New York, NY: Facts on File, 2004.

Crawford, Matthew B. *Shop Class as Soul Craft: An Inquiry into the Value of Work*. New York, NY: Penguin Books, 2010.

Freedman, Jeri. *Electrician* (Careers in Construction). New York, NY: Cavendish Square, 2016.

Harmon, Daniel E. *A Career as an Electrician* (Essential Careers). New York, NY: Rosen Publishing, 2010.

Lew, Kristi, and Kezia Endsley. *Engineer* (Careers in Construction). New York, NY: Cavendish Square, 2016.

McKeon, John K. *Becoming a Construction Manager*. Hoboken, NJ: John Wiley, 2011.

Reeves, Ellen Gordon. *Can I Wear My Nose Ring to the Interview? A Crash Course in Finding, Landing, and Keeping Your First Real Job*. New York, NY: Workman Publishing Company, Inc., 2009.

Schauer, Peter J., and Kezia Endsley. *General Contractor* (Careers in Construction). New York, NY: Cavendish Square, 2016.

Small, Cathleen. *Carpenter* (Careers in Construction). New York, NY: Cavendish Square, 2016.

Toth, Henrietta. *A Career as a Heavy Equipment Operator* (Essential Careers). New York, NY: Rosen Publishing, 2016.

Wolny, Philip. *Getting a Job in Building Maintenance (Job Basics)*. New York, NY: Rosen Publishing, 2014.

Wolny, Philip. *Money-Making Opportunities for Teens Who Are Handy*. New York, NY: Rosen Publishing, 2014.

"Best Construction Jobs: Construction Worker." *U.S. News & World Report*. Retrieved January 15, 2016 (http://money.usnews.com/careers/best-jobs/construction-worker).

Bureau of Labor Statistics. "How to Become a Masonry Worker." Retrieved January 15, 2016 (http://www.bls.gov/ooh/construction-and-extraction/brickmasons-blockmasons-and-stonemasons.htm#tab-4).

Bureau of Labor Statistics. "Occupational Outlook Handbook: Construction and Extraction Occupations." Retrieved January 15, 2016 (http://www.bls.gov/ooh/construction-and-extraction/home.htm).

Haring, Bob. "Differences Between a Journeyman and a Master Electrician." *Houston Chronicle*. Retrieved January 15, 2016 (http://work.chron.com/differences-between-journeyman-master-electrician-2158.html).

Jackson, Barbara J. *Construction Management Jump Start: The Best First Step Toward a Career in Construction Management*. Indianapolis, IN: Wiley & Sons, 2010.

Lang, Robert W. "There is Hope for High School Woodworking Programs." Popularwoodworking.com, June 2, 2014. Retrieved January 15, 2016 (http://www.popularwoodworking.com/woodworking-blogs/editors-blog/hope-high-school-woodworking-programs).

National Center for Education Statistics. "Fast Facts: Income of Young Adults." Retrieved January 15, 2016 (http://nces.ed.gov/fastfacts/display.asp?id=77).

Sheftell, Jason. "Building School: Learn the Art of Construction at a top Brooklyn Trade Academy." *Daily News*, January 14, 2010. Retrieved January 15, 2016 (http://www.nydailynews.com/life-style/real-estate/

building-school-learn-art-construction-top-brooklyn-trade-academy-article-1.458924).

Sumichrast, Michael. *Opportunities in Building Construction Careers*. New York, NY: McGraw Hill, 2007.

Sumichrast, Michael. *Opportunities in Building Construction Trades*. New York, NY: McGraw Hill, 1998.

United States Department of Labor Employment and Training Administration. "What is Registered Apprenticeship?" Retrieved January 10, 2016 (https://www.doleta.gov/oa/apprenticeship.cfm).

A

apprenticeships, 6
  age requirements for, 47
  duration of, 46
  on-the-job, 40–45
  registered, 45–47

B

blueprints, 17, 39, 41
brickmason, 6, 16, 41, 46

C

career and technical education
    (CTE), 25
career counselor, 27–28
carpenter, 6, 17–18, 27, 39, 46, 50
cement mason, 6, 16, 41
community college, 25, 33, 34, 39, 45
construction work
  demands of, 11–12, 15, 16, 18, 23
  education for, 6, 14–15, 24–35,
    36–47
  getting a job in, 48–59
  mental pressures of, 12
  on-the-job conduct, 60–69
  outlook for, 69
  physical condition for, 9, 16, 18,
    21, 22
  private projects, 7
  public works, 7
  requirements for, 7–11, 15–23

salaries for, 46
specialization in, 23, 41
technical skills for, 17
types of jobs, 5–6, 7, 15–23
counseling, 27–28

D

demolition, 22–23
drywall, 6, 18, 39

E

education, 6, 14–15, 24–35
electrician, 5, 6, 21, 27, 46
  journeyman, 42–45
employment websites, 49–50
engineer, 5
explosives, 23

F

financial aid, 34–35
foremen, 12, 33, 57, 66

G

General Educational Development
    (GED), 14
glassworker, 6
glazier, 6
"green building," 31
guidance counselor, 27–28, 48

About the Author

Philip Wolny is a writer and editor from Queens, New York City. He has written many career-related titles for Rosen Publishing, including *Getting a Job in Building Maintenance* and *Money-making Opportunities for Teens Who are Handy*.

Photo Credits